The Welsh quarries in the 1950s, with 'Cloister', built by Hunslet Ltd of Leeds in 1891, picking her way carefully over poor track at Dinorwic Quarries, Llanberis. 'Cloister' is a typical example of the numerous Hunslet saddle tank engines used in Wales: the lack of cab was due to tight clearances in tunnels, the short wheelbase permitted use on tightly curved track, while the wooden buffers prevented 'buffer locking' on such curves.

INDUSTRIAL
NARROW GAUGE RAILWAYS

Ian Dean

Shire Publications Ltd

CONTENTS

Published by Shire Publications Ltd, Midland House, West Way, Botley, Oxford OX2 0PH. Copyright © 2003 by Ian Dean. First published 1985; reprinted 1990, 1998 and 2003. Transferred to digital print on demand 2011. Shire Library 145. ISBN 978 0 85263 752 4.

Printed in Great Britain by PrintOnDemand-Worldwide.com, Peterborough, UK.

ACKNOWLEDGEMENTS
I would like to thank my colleagues at Amberley Working Museum, the Members of the Railway Group, Sheila Land (Honorary Librarian) and particularly David Smith (Trustee), for their help in preparing this book. My thanks are also due to my wife, Julie, for her patience and cups of coffee during late evening sessions at the typewriter. Photographs on the following pages are acknowledged to: Amberley Working Museum Library, pages 8, 9, 12, 14, 15 (lower), 22 (lower), 24, 25, 26 (lower); Bicton Woodland Railway, page 28 (lower); A. W. Deller, page 17 (lower); C. G. Down, page 20 (lower); Festiniog Railway, pages 5, 18; A. Fisher (LBNGR), page 4; Alan Keef Ltd, page 29; J. B. Latham Collection, page 3, 21; Lister & Company, page 13; L. G. Marshall, pages 17 (upper), 19, 23 (lower); John H. Meredith, page 15 (upper), 20 (upper); National Coal Board, page 6 (lower); M. F, Portsmouth, page 7; David H. Smith, pages 10, 11, 16, 22 (upper), 23 (upper), 26 (upper), 28 (upper); Thomas Smith (Rodley) Ltd, page 6 (upper); Talyllyn Railway, page 2, 27; Michael E. Ware, page 1.

Cover: Alice, a Hunslet 0-4-0 ST built in 1902, was originally operated in the Dinorwic slate quarries at Llanberis, North Wales. She normally resides at the Bala Lake Railway, but is shown here working at Leighton Buzzard Light Railway. (Photograph courtesy of Steve Makin)

Talyllyn Railway, about 1890, with Number 2 Dolgoch at Tywyn Wharf. Note the stacks of slate in the background, the track ballasted up almost to rail-top level, and the clothes – it may have been a Sunday excursion.

A contractor's line in use during the building of the Guildford bypass in the 1930s. The locomotive is an 0-6-0 well tank owned by Surrey County Council and built by Hudswell Clarke.

HISTORY OF THE NARROW GAUGE

Railways originated as a result of the need to provide a track to lift wheeled vehicles above the mud of the road surface. The track on these early 'tramroads' might be made from wood, stone or iron. Wooden wagons running on wooden rails and drawn by horses were in use by the sixteenth century. The wooden rails, however, became worn away by the weather and by continual use, and strips of iron were later added to the upper surfaces of the rails to extend their life. During the eighteenth century iron rails were introduced and the gauge (or width between the rails) was set at around 4 feet (1219 mm), the space within which a horse could walk comfortably.

The north-east of England is the region usually associated with the development of the first railways, but the first public goods railway in the world was in the south-east. The Surrey Iron Railway opened on 26th July 1803 from Wandsworth to Croydon, using iron rails supported on stone blocks, and with a track gauge of just over 4 feet (1219 mm). By 1812 the first commercially used steam locomotive was running on the Middleton

Colliery Railway in Leeds, and three years later George Stephenson had built a locomotive for Killingworth Colliery that would haul 50 tons at 6 miles (10 km) an hour on the level. This was the beginning of the great railway mania, but it was not until after 1830 that the horse gave way more widely to the steam locomotive for haulage as the use of railways spread rapidly through Britain.

The track gauge of 4 feet 8½ inches (1435 mm) soon became regarded as the 'standard' gauge, although the 7 foot 0¼ inch (2140 mm) gauge of I. K. Brunel's Great Western Railway was preferred by many. The last of the 'broad gauge' trains on the Great Western Railway ran in 1892 and the system was brought into line with the other British railway companies. The problems of interchange of both passengers and goods between the two gauges brought this conversion about — a problem that was to occur with the narrow gauge too.

In parallel with the development of this national network of major railways, numerous tramroads and minor railways were continuing to serve industry, and

3

many of these were of a narrower gauge than the main lines. Most of the narrow gauge lines came into being in the nineteenth century, to move loads with greater ease, reliability and economy than could be achieved with the contemporary alternatives — the wheelbarrow and the horse-drawn cart or wagon. In bad weather it would have been almost impossible to move a useful load by these means, especially in a quarry or on a contractor's site.

Narrow gauge railways developed to meet local needs and conditions, with over thirty nominally different gauges existing throughout Great Britain, varying between 1 foot 3 inches (381 mm) and 4 feet 6 inches (1372 mm). In the pioneering days the gauge varied from site to site because of the lack of manufacturing standardisation, the lack of communication between neighbouring purchasers, and the idiosyncrasies of consulting engineers. Moreover before the widespread development of main-line railways the minor lines served the nearest waterway. At the waterside wharf the load had to be transferred from railway wagon to canal boat, and there was therefore no need for standardisation of gauges between neighbouring systems.

A purchaser who chose the narrow gauge for his railway often did so for financial reasons. The lighter rolling stock and motive power needed rail of a lighter weight, which in turn allowed the use of lighter wooden sleepers. The rail could be bent more easily around sharper curves, the gradient changes could be greater, and the components and their delivery to the site were therefore cheaper than for an equivalent length of standard gauge line. Furthermore, in the case of a quarry or other type of temporary working the tracks could easily be lifted and relaid elsewhere to cope with a new source of raw material.

Today the use of crawler-tracked or wheeled earth-moving machinery is widespread, but in the past any major constructional work required the building of a temporary railway by the contractor, to carry supplies and remove spoil. Before the First World War most contractors would have a fleet of locomotives and wagons, usually of around 3 foot (914 mm) gauge, and these would be moved from job to job as needed, much in the way that modern plant is.

The First World War brought a significant change in direction of the development of narrow gauge railways. At the

A train of skip wagons emptying sand into the drying plant at Garsides Ltd, Leighton Buzzard. A Motor-Rail diesel is at the head of the train, on part of the line that now forms the Leighton Buzzard Narrow Gauge Railway.

The Festiniog Railway, Gwynedd: a scene that is almost undatable but is in preservation days. 'Prince', an 0-4-0 saddle tank by George England Ltd, shunts Minfford exchange sidings with a ballast train.

end of the war a considerable amount of war surplus material in the form of steam, petrol and electric locomotives, rolling stock and track came on to the market, the vast majority of this equipment being of nominal 2 foot (600 mm) gauge. This availability of reasonably priced material brought about a rapid change by industrial and contracting users, the primary narrow gauge quickly becoming 2 feet.

The narrow gauge railway was developed in a quest for greater industrial efficiency, and the demise of lines came about for the same reason. It has now become more economic to use conveyor belts, overhead cableways or special rough terrain vehicles than to use a railway, except in a few special cases such as when tunnelling or when working over soft ground, for example on peat bogs. Therefore during the 1960s and 1970s the

number of working lines declined dramatically, and only a few are still regularly active.

This decline was, however, matched by a growing interest in the preservation of industrial equipment and in the surviving lines themselves. As steam operation ended on British Railways, enthusiasts turned their attention to the surviving industrial lines and to other narrow gauge lines that were still at work or were pioneers of the preservation movement. The Talyllyn and Festiniog railways in North Wales were the first such lines to be run by enthusiasts, using the track and equipment of the previous operators. Since those early days of the preservation movement many other lines have been reopened or created anew using locomotives and rolling stock that formerly saw industrial use.

5

ABOVE: *A dragline excavator filling hand-propelled skip wagons in a sand pit at Buckden, Cambridgeshire, in 1934.*

BELOW: *An underground diesel mines locomotive at work at Bates Colliery, Northumberland, in 1960, hauling a train of 3½ ton capacity mine cars. Diesel locomotives operating underground are fitted with special equipment to purify the exhaust and to prevent the emission of sparks or flames.*

Heavy horse haulage in 1934; the then modern excavator provides a startling contrast. The River Severn Catchment Board, who were undertaking this work, had yet to acquire their first locomotive.

MOTIVE POWER

MANUAL

Man provided the earliest form of motive power himself, and in some cases he still does today. It was quickly found that far heavier loads could be moved on rails, even when propelled by hand, because of the reduced friction. Only single wagons were usually moved by this method of propulsion. In the small private coal mines of South Wales and the Forest of Dean hand-worked lines still survive, and at Charlton, near Chichester in West Sussex, a complete sawmill is served by such a system.

HORSE

To provide increased tractive effort the next logical step was to harness a horse to the wagon. The horse was usually 'loose coupled' to a train of several wagons by chains, some of the wagons being fitted with primitive brakes to halt their progress when necessary. On the Festiniog Railway, built to a gauge of 1 foot 11½ inches (597 mm), loaded wagons of slate were coupled into trains and allowed to run down by gravity from the quarries in the hills, the horses riding in special wagons. After the wagons were unloaded the horses were used to haul them back up the gradient to the quarries. A few horse-worked lines survive today, mostly at private coal mines.

CABLE AND CHAIN

Many industrial works used a large stationary steam, gas or oil engine to power the machinery in the works buildings, and in some cases this source of power was utilised in conjunction with a narrow gauge railway. In a cable haulage system the wagons were usually semi-permanently attached to a moving steel cable and were loaded and tipped on the move. With chain haulage a wagon could be attached at will to the moving chain by engaging a link into the V-shaped projection on the top of any wagon. Cable haulage was also used on the inclined planes which linked the different working levels in some quarries. At the brickworks of Redland Ltd at North Holmwood, Surrey, a cable-operated incline powered by a stationary engine hauled

7

ABOVE: *Loading clay at North Holmwood brickworks, Surrey, in the 1980s. The battery-electric locomotive takes the loaded train to the foot of the incline.*
BELOW: *Having arrived at the foot of the incline the loaded wagons were hauled up by cable to the top, where they were tipped into the machinery inside the works.*

8

A Motor-Rail 'Simplex', dating from the First World War, at the head of a pair of skips at Amberley Working Museum. Restored in 1980, this locomotive formerly worked at the City of Chichester sewage works.

loaded skip wagons up the incline that fed the clay into the works, the loaded wagons having been deposited at the foot of the incline by semi-automatically operated battery-electric locomotives — an interesting combination.

INTERNAL COMBUSTION ENGINE

The internal combustion engine, fuelled by petrol, paraffin or oil has been used in locomotives from the beginning of the twentieth century to the present day. Richard Hornsby and Sons Ltd, of Grantham, built the first commercially successful oil-engined locomotives between 1896 and 1903. Six engines were built, powered by the Hornsby-Ackroyd patent oil engine. The first was of 9½ horsepower and ran on the 18 inch gauge (457 mm) system at the Woolwich Arsenal explosives factory.

The greatest period of development took place during the First World War. John Dixon-Abbott designed a gearbox with two speeds in both forward and reverse, the engine and gearbox sitting transversely in the locomotive frame and driving both axles by roller chains. The design and experimental work was carried out at the Phoenix Ironworks, Lewes, East Sussex, by the Motor Rail and Tram Car Company Ltd. Production was moved to Bedford, and over one thousand 'tractors' were made for the War Department light railways, most of which served in France on the lines laid between the standard gauge railheads and the front. Their reliability did much to ensure the future of the internal combustion engine as an alternative to the steam engine, which had until then predominated on the narrow gauge.

In the 1930s reliable and easy-to-start oil engines began to become available in sizes varying from 10 up to several hundred horsepower, and some locomotives were fitted with these, using chain, hydraulic or electric drive. Most used engines specially developed for the purpose, but some manufacturers used road vehicle engines adapted to rail use. Hudson Ltd, of Leeds, built a locomotive based on the four-cylinder power unit of a Fordson Standard agricultural tractor. This was started using petrol as the fuel, but as the engine warmed up a tap was turned and the engine then ran on the cheaper TVO (tractor vapourising oil). In the 1950s Fowler Ltd, also of Leeds, built a locomotive based on the Field Marshall agricultural tractor engine, a large horizontal single-cylinder oil-fuelled unit.

9

A 'Planet' type locomotive, built by the Kent Construction Company of Ashford, Kent, in the 1920s. One of the few types built in south-east England, it was originally fitted with a Meadows four-cylinder petrol engine of a type used in some vintage sporting cars.

ELECTRICITY

The use of electric locomotives drawing their current from overhead wires or ground-level conductor rails was unusual in industry in Great Britain. The danger of accidents from the conductors was a serious problem, and the lack of flexibility when moving temporary lines was an added disadvantage.

During the First World War a number of 'petrol-electric' locomotives were built. The petrol engine drove a dynamo that provided the current for the traction motor. One advantage of this type was that it could be used to haul a mobile workshop train. On arrival at the working area the train would be halted and the dynamo would feed electricity to power the lathes, drills and other machines in the workshops. This type of propulsion was not developed fully until the introduction of the diesel engine, and then only in larger locomotives.

An interesting conversion, undertaken in 1927 at the Llechwedd Slate Mines in North Wales, was the adaptation of a conventional steam locomotive (a Bagnall-built 0-4-0 saddle tank) to electrical power, with current collection by overhead wire. This conversion was undertaken in the quarries' own workshops, and the locomotive survived in operation into the 1970s.

One way to overcome the problems of current supply is for the electric locomotive to carry its own current in batteries. The battery electric is considered by many operators to be an ideal machine, cheap to run, easy to drive, economical to maintain and sparing on fuel, as it uses electricity only when moving. The battery pack is carried on the frame of the locomotive, providing weight for added traction, and in some instances it is detachable and can be exchanged quickly for a fully charged spare, thereby extending the availability of the locomotive for use. The batteries are usually recharged overnight in the engine shed, often using cheaper 'off-peak' electricity.

Redland Brick Ltd had a number of battery electrics in use at its North

ABOVE: *Two examples of the product of the Motor Rail and Tramcar Company Ltd of Bedford, at work in 1979 at the Marlow Sand and Gravel Company's pit. The engine on the left, Number 3, was built in 1934, and that on the right, Number 4, in 1943.*

BELOW: *Two chain-driven four-wheeled diesels, both built in 1937. The Orenstein and Koppel (left) has a vertical single-cylinder engine, and the Ransomes and Rapier (right) has a more conventional Ailsa Craig twin-cylinder type. The Ransomes and Rapier is the only known survivor of the make. Both may be seen on display at Amberley Working Museum.*

ABOVE: *Two four-wheeled diesels: a Hudson-Hunslet built in 1941 for the Ministry of Supply (left) and a Ruston and Hornsby 16/20 horsepower built in 1937 and formerly used at Naburn Sewage Works, York (right). Both are now at Amberley Working Museum.*

BELOW: *Tilmanstone Colliery in Kent was the home of this Hudswell-Clarke 'mines' type locomotive built in 1948, seen here waiting restoration at Amberley Working Museum. Powered by a Gardner 4LW oil engine with air brakes, this powerful locomotive weighs 11 tons.*

A lightweight diesel locomotive on test at the manufacturers, Lister and Company, of Dursley, Gloucestershire. Listers are renowned for their stationary engines and for a small factory vehicle known as the 'Auto-truck'. Their first rail vehicles, of the 1930s, were based on this petrol-engined truck.

Holmwood works until 1981. These locomotives were fitted with automatic control gear actuated by ramps on the track, and they operated without a driver. The locomotive would be coupled to its train and set in motion by a workman standing alongside the engine. The train would proceed along the track and when it reached the 'stop' ramp the power would be shut off and the brakes automatically applied. The sight of the driverless train approaching round a bend was an awe-inspiring sight for the unsuspecting visitor.

The battery electric is ideal for mining and tunnelling work, because it produces no fumes.

COMPRESSED AIR

This source of motive power was little used in Great Britain. Some underground mine locomotives were built in the late nineteenth century, but all were out of use by 1900. In Germany and the United States of America more use was made of compressed air as a source of power, and

a number of engines continued to be built into the 1960s. A large air receiver, filled from a stationary compressor, was mounted on a chassis similar to that of a steam locomotive. The air operated cylinders and valve gear, which were coupled to the driving wheels. The operational advantage was that no heat, sparks or fumes were produced, but the working range was limited by the capacity of the air receiver.

STEAM

The steam engine is the power source most often associated with narrow gauge railways.

The requirements of industrial locomotives were different in many ways from those of their standard counterparts. Industrials needed to carry less water and fuel, as their journeys were usually short and supplies were close at hand. The locomotives were therefore generally 'tank' engines (that is they carried their own water on the engine itself, rather than towing a separate tender for coal

13

A four-wheel battery-electric locomotive built by Wingrove and Rogers Ltd of Liverpool. This model, the WR5, at 1½ tons is the lightest in a range extending up to 8 tons. It is powered by a 48 volt battery pack and available in gauges from 18 to 24 inches (457 to 610 mm).

and water). The locomotives needed to be rugged, simple to maintain, and simple to operate. For this reason the cylinders were usually mounted outside the frames, but the valve gear was usually placed between the frames where it was less likely to suffer accidental damage. Stability on poor track was important and many types of locomotive carried their water in tanks between the mainframes. This lowered the centre of gravity and helped keep the engine from turning on its side, but it limited the amount of water that could be carried. Locomotives of this type were known as 'well tanks' but the most common type was the 'saddle tank', in which the water was carried in a tank set astride the boiler, as the name suggests.

To ensure that the maximum weight was available for traction, most designs did not use leading or trailing trucks, the 0-4-0 and 0-6-0 being the most common types. (0-4-0 denotes a locomotive with no leading wheels, four driving wheels and no trailing wheels, 0-6-0 one with six

driving wheels but no leading or trailing wheels.) Some 0-6-0 designs were built with flangeless centre driving wheels to allow sharper curves to be negotiated with a fixed wheelbase.

To give a greater hauling power, articulated locomotives were sometimes built, such as the Fairlie 0-4-4-0 tank engines on the Festiniog Railway. These had two boilers, two sets of cylinders, two chimneys: virtually everything except the crew was duplicated. Other designs were constructed, such as the Beyer-Garratt, the Mallet, the Shay and the Climax, but few operated in Great Britain. The Shay and the Climax were commonest in the USA, where they were used principally in the logging industry. The advantage of articulation was the ability of one locomotive to cope with much greater loads, with no extra crew, and without having to ease the existing sharp curves to accommodate a fixed wheelbase type of equivalent power.

Other variations included vertical-boiler 'coffee-pot' type locomotives, such as

14

ABOVE: *A vertical-boilered 0-4-0 called 'Watkin' built by De Winton in 1893, seen here in 1950 working for the Penmaenmawr and Welsh Granite Company, North Wales. The driver stood on the left-hand end of the footplate, the water tank and cylinders being placed at the opposite end. The brake, regulator, reverser and gauge glass can be clearly seen.*

BELOW: *This 0-4-0 is a typical example of a British four-wheeled well-tank locomotive, built by Andrew Barclay Ltd of Kilmarnock in 1931. It served as Number 70 on the Dinorwic Quarries lines in North Wales before moving to the Hollycombe Steam Collection, Hampshire, and acquiring the name 'Caledonia'.*

15

The Penrhyn Castle Museum houses this amazing survivor, 'Fire Queen', constructed by A. Horlock of Northfleet in 1848 for the 4 foot (1219 mm) gauge Padarn Railway, North Wales. The railway connected the Dinorwic Quarry with Port Dinorwic 6½ miles (10.5 km) away on the coast. Sister engine 'Jenny Lind' was scrapped in 1886, but 'Fire Queen' survived in a shed at Gilfach Ddu, to be restored and placed on display. The notable features include the lack of frame, a long wheelbase, and wooden boiler cladding.

ABOVE: *On the unusual gauge of 3 feet 2¹/₄ inches (972 mm), 'Townsend Hook' is seen at the Betchworth quarries of the Dorking Greystone Lime Company in Surrey. Built in 1880 by Fletcher Jennings of Whitehaven, this is a good example of a side-tanked engine. It is seen here drawing loaded wagons away from the incline to the lime kilns. 'Townsend Hook' may now be seen at Amberley Working Museum.*

BELOW: *'Scaldwell' was built in 1913 for the Scaldwell Ironstone Quarries, Northamptonshire, by Peckett and Company of Bristol. This 3 foot (914 mm) gauge system closed in 1963 and 'Scaldwell' was rescued by the former Brockham Museum.*

'Linda', an 0-4-0 saddle tank built for the Penrhyn Quarry Railway in 1893 by the Hunslet Engine Company of Leeds. Seen here after purchase by the Festiniog Railway in 1962, she is now used regularly on passenger trains, having been fitted with a leading pair of wheels and a tender for the oil fuel with which she is now fired.

those by De Winton, and the more recent vertically boilered types produced by Sentinel Ltd. One Sentinel example, built in 1926 for the Kettering Iron and Coal Company, was an articulated type, with two vertical boilers.

A type which found little favour generally was the 'fireless' locomotive. The fireless engine consisted of a normal steam engine chassis and running gear, with the boiler replaced by a reservoir resembling a boiler without a chimney. This was charged with high-pressure steam from a stationary source, such as a factory boiler. This type could operate for about four hours on a charge of steam and was ideal for use in places such as

paper mills or explosives factories where the risk of sparks could not be taken. They had the further advantage that they carried no fuel or water, but their main disadvantages were the limited range of operation and the reliance on an external steam source.

Many fine examples of industrial steam locomotives survive in preservation, operating on the lines under enthusiast management or at steam centres around Great Britain. Although the cost of maintaining old steam engines is high, it is proportionate to their size, and a small industrial engine can be re-boilered more cheaply than a massive standard gauge express locomotive.

ABOVE: *Locomotives were exported to the colonies and some are still at work. 'Joan' is an 0-4-0 saddle tank built by Bagnall of Stafford in 1924. Photographed in 1978 at a colliery in Assam, India, she shows signs of a long and hard working life, with patches on her cab and saddle tank, twisted cab, steps and buffer beam. Lumps of clay seal holes in the smokebox around the base of the chimney.*
BELOW: *More veterans at work in India in 1984 at the Upper India Sugar Mills, near Delhi. The 0-6-0 well tank (left) was built by Fowler of Leeds and the 4-6-0T 'Lion' (right) was built during the First World War by Baldwin in the USA and supplied to the British Army for service on the '2 foot' (600 mm) railways supplying the front lines. Both locomotives have now returned to the UK for restoration.*

ABOVE: *A four-wheeled vertical-boilered locomotive, built by Sentinel of Shrewsbury in 1929, and seen working on the 2 foot 11 inch (889 mm) gauge line at the London Brick Company's works at Fletton, Peterborough. The boiler is situated in the cab, the cylinders are under the 'bonnet' and the drive to the axles is by chain.*

BELOW: *'Unique', a fireless engine built in 1923 by Bagnall of Stafford for the Bowaters paper mill at Sittingbourne. It was charged with steam from a high-pressure source at the power house and could run for up to eight hours on one charging. 'Unique' is now on static display at the Sittingbourne and Kemsley Light Railway.*

Two wagons at the Betchworth, Surrey, premises of the Dorking Greystone Lime Company. These end-tipping wagons were built on site using bought-in wheels and bearings.

ROLLING STOCK

Wagons could either be purchased from the stocks of a limited number of types held by the manufacturers, such as Bagnall of Stafford or Hudson of Leeds, or were built 'in house' by some works engineers, who bought axles and bearings and then built their own wagons to suit local needs, a carpenter making the chassis and body, and a blacksmith providing the metal strapping and the fittings such as hinges and couplings. Although some of the wooden wagons looked very primitive, they were usually carefully made for ease of working, the design having been worked out over a long period of use and experimentation. Tipping wagons could easily be emptied by one man, and wagons used on inclines had to have a low centre of gravity to aid stability. Many of these wooden wagons were rebuilt time and again over many years, the original metalwork being reused on new timbers, but to the old and well tried designs. Two wagons that looked identical could have been built as much as seventy-five years apart.

The most common type of wagon is the 'skip', a side-tipping wagon with a V-shaped body, both body and chassis being made of steel. These were built by a number of manufacturers and produced in various carrying capacities.

Each industry required special wagons. Brickworks needed skips for carrying clay and flat cars with racks for carrying the bricks through the drying tunnels. The paper industry called for large-capacity bogie flat cars to carry the wood pulp. Coal mines needed big metal wagons that could withstand rough handling. The slate industry needed a variety of types to carry slabs of slate, finished roofing slates and the waste which was taken to the tips. The peat industry required lightweight wagons of high carrying capacity to carry their light load. The variety was enormous and contributed to the individuality of the different locations.

The carriage of passengers on industrial systems provided further interest in the variety of stock used. Some lines such as the Festiniog provided 'quarrymen's coaches', four-wheeled coaches that were roofed and provided very basic comforts. However, the Penrhyn Quarry provided only open coaches for the quarrymen. In some instances makeshift seats were placed across the sides of slate wagons or seats were fitted to skip-wagon chassis. Passenger comfort was not the prime consideration and regulations governing operation were minimal.

21

As most of the industrial lines existed to convey goods and not passengers, few industrial coaches survive on the preserved lines, with the exception of the Festiniog and Talyllyn railways. Some railways, such as the now defunct Lincoln-shire Coast Light Railway, made use of Hudson bogie vans dating from the First World War and converted them to passenger coaches. Others have had to build new vehicles.

ABOVE: *A brick-clay wagon from the 2 foot 11 inch (889 mm) gauge line at the London Brick Company's works at Arlesey. Now on display at Amberley Working Museum.*

BELOW: *A selection of slate quarrying wagons. From left: Oakeley Quarry slate rubbish wagon; Dinorwic Quarry incline slab wagon; Penrhyn Quarry fullersite wagon; Dinorwic Quarry coal wagon; London and North Western Railway 2 ton slate wagon.*

ABOVE: *Skip wagons have been produced in many sizes and forms over the years by many manufacturers, although all to a basically similar design. The largest supplier was Hudson of Leeds, but this example is a product of one of the smaller manufacturers — Whites Ltd of Widnes.*
BELOW: *Three narrow gauge skips are being carried on the standard gauge transporter wagon that linked two hand-operated lines at the kilns and hydrator of the Dorking Greystone Lime Company. The standard gauge locomotive is a vertical-boilered 0-4-0 by Head, Wrightson of Middlesbrough, built in 1871.*

ABOVE: *A chain-haulage wagon. Note the V-shaped clip in which the chain locates.*

BELOW: *A 5 ton mine car from Tilmanstone Colliery, Kent, fitted with automatic couplings and roller-bearing axleboxes. Used underground in the coal mine, it was acquired by Amberley Working Museum, along with a matching Hudswell-Clarke locomotive.*

A very basic passenger coach, from the 18 inch (457 mm) gauge system within the Royal Arsenal at Woolwich.

Hudson of Leeds built this bogie passenger coach in 1940 for use on the 2 foot (610 mm) gauge line at RAF Fauld in Staffordshire. It is now completely renovated and in use on passenger trains at Amberley Working Museum.

A passenger car for important visitors, used at the Dinorwic Quarry, North Wales. Note the double-flanged wheels and the sloping seats for added comfort on the inclined tracks. This vehicle is on display at the Hollycombe Steam Collection, Liphook, Hampshire.

ABOVE: *A typical example of industrial trackwork, at Manod Quarry, North Wales, at the foot of an incline. The right-hand track leads to a point for the double-flanged wheels; note the cast iron 'blades' and the switchable 'frog'. The track on the left ends in a 'spoon' point; the rails are lifted over on top of those on the right for operation. The rail is principally flat-bottom, but the blades of the 'spoon' consist of one piece of bridge-rail and one oddment of steel that the blacksmith has made up to match. Note the incline chain in the top left of the picture.*

LEFT: *Bull-headed rail rescued from Dinorwic Quarry, North Wales, on display at Hollycombe Steam Collection, Liphook, Hampshire. This shows a stub point; the photograph below shows the switchable frog. This is a sturdier version of the point shown above for use by locomotives.*

Still at work on the line it was built for in 1866, 'Dolgoch' is Number 2 on the Talyllyn Railway, seen here with a train of original coaches between Tywyn Wharf and Pendre.

THE TRACK

Track in the earliest days consisted either of timber 'rails' or of timber with strips of iron added on the top surface to increase the life of the timber members. The next development was the use of iron rails supported on stone blocks at each joint, as on the Surrey Iron Railway. This led to the adoption of iron rails on wooden sleepers, and finally to steel rails on wooden or metal sleepers.

The weight of the rails varied from 14 pounds per yard (6.9 kg/m) to 90 pounds per yard (45 kg/m), with the average weight per yard being around 35 to 40 pounds (17 to 20 kg/m). During the First World War 'Jubilee' track, made in panels with metal sleepers in straight sections and curves of varying radii, was much used. Points were also made in the same manner, and with these components lines could be laid quickly and repaired quickly if damaged by shell fire. These panels have survived well and many can still be found in use, with either 14 pound (6.9 kg/m) or 20 pound (10 kg/m) rail.

Most lines used flat-bottom rail spiked direct to wooden sleepers, but some used bull-head rail in cast-iron chairs, the rail being held in place by tapered wooden keys.

The quality of trackwork varied enormously. On a system that was worked by hand, the route at points might be changed by kicking each rail over with a boot, whereas on a steam-operated line that also handled passengers there would be point levers and rodding up to main-line standard. Most industrial lines followed the existing levels of the land with a minimum of earthworks, ballast and maintenance. Derailments were not uncommon, and on some lines the spilled loads from derailed wagons could be seen along the lineside. Most locomotives carried jacks for putting them back on the rails. However, despite the state of the track, there were seldom any serious accidents. The track of several systems still working in the 1970s was in a poor condition: often the rails were not visible, but an oily trail along the grass would indicate where the foliage had brushed against the sump of a locomotive.

ABOVE: *'Chaloner', a vertical-boilered De Winton locomotive built in 1877, seen here in its centenary year at work on the Leighton Buzzard Narrow Gauge Railway. 'Chaloner' formerly worked at the Pen-yr-Orsedd Slate Quarry, Nantlle, North Wales.*

BELOW: *'Woolwich', an 0-4-0T built by the Avonside Engine Company to 18 inch (457 mm) gauge for the Royal Arsenal at Woolwich. It was photographed at the Bicton Woodland Railway in Devon but is now at the Royal Gunpowder Mills, Waltham Abbey, Essex.*

One company still actively building narrow gauge equipment is Alan Keef Ltd. Here a Keef K12 diesel is at work on a peat railway. The company produces a range of locomotives, from this 14 horsepower model up to the 62 horsepower model K60. The haulage capacity for the K12 is around 30 tons on level track, with power provided by an air-cooled twin-cylinder oil engine.

THE NARROW GAUGE TODAY

The first preservation project in Great Britain was the rescue of the Talyllyn Railway in North Wales in 1950. The line was taken over as a going concern, never having closed, but the locomotives, rolling stock and buildings were very run-down. The new operators struggled through the pioneering days and proved that enthusiasm was the vital factor, and this encouraged others to consider new challenges elsewhere. Shortly after the Talyllyn had come under new management a preservation society was formed to reopen the nearby Festiniog Railway, which had been closed since 1946. The Festiniog Railway was reopened in stages from Porthmadog to Blaenau Ffestiniog, the final section being brought into use in 1983. A new route had to be taken on the upper section above Dduallt to avoid a reservoir constructed while the line was disused. This deviation from the original course of the line required a loop to lift the line to a new and higher level and the cutting of a tunnel at Moelwyn. A lengthy court case was necessary to claim compensation from the reservoir builders.

Other lines have since been partially reopened, including the Welshpool and Llanfair Light Railway, the Welsh Highland Railway and a short stretch of the Corris Railway. Several new pleasure systems have been created on the track-work of old industrial systems, such as the Sittingbourne and Kemsley, in Kent, which uses the equipment and track of a paper mill. The lines laid to serve Garside's and Arnold's sand pits at Leighton Buzzard now form the Leighton Buzzard Narrow Gauge Railway. Several of the petrol and diesel-engined locomotives are still used for passenger and works trains, having been acquired from the former owners, but a number of industrial steam engines are regularly operated too.

New railways have been built using equipment formerly used in industry, either on completely new sites, or in some instances on the trackbed of former standard gauge lines closed by British Rail. The Lincolnshire Coast Light Railway (now closed) was created using materials and stock acquired from Nocton, Lincolnshire, where it had been used by the makers of Smith's Crisps to serve their extensive potato farms. The track, wagons and petrol-engined locomotives date from the First World War. They had been acquired at surplus sales after the war and were disposed of when road haulage superseded the railway. At Bicton Park in Devon an attractive line was created using track and stock purchased from the Royal Arsenal at Woolwich, where there had been extensive narrow and standard gauge systems serving the explosives factories.

Tourist attractions such as Hollycombe, near Liphook, Hampshire, and Whipsnade Zoo, Bedfordshire, realised the value of having a passenger-carrying railway, and several such venues installed railways using former industrial locomotives. Many short private lines were created by small groups of people purely for their own pleasure.

Another type of operation is that centred around a museum, either purely railway orientated, or as part of a more widely based collection. The Brockham Museum, created in a former limeworks quarry in the North Downs near Dorking, Surrey, was an excellent example of such a project. It was a bold attempt to create a working museum of industrial and narrow gauge railways, set up in 1962 by members of the Narrow Gauge Railway Society. Much hard work was done on the site and on the collection by the team of volunteers, but there were insurmountable problems over planning and vehicle access to the site, and the trustees decided to seek an alternative home for the collection. They found that their aspirations blended with those of the trustees of the Southern Industrial History Centre, based at Amberley Working Museum in West Sussex, and the two collections were merged in 1982. There is now a fine display of material on show at Amberley.

A few lines continue in industrial use, and some builders still produce locomotives, rolling stock and track. It is still possible to see a diesel locomotive and train of skip wagons trundling over poorly laid track, a survivor from another era. These survivors are few and far between, economics and lack of flexibility having long since brought about the closure of most of these systems in favour of the dump truck or conveyor. Various societies have recorded details of virtually everything that does remain, and very few items go to the scrapyard now.

Developments are still taking place to improve the efficiency and ease of operation of steam locomotives. New locomotives have been built closely following industrial designs. Locomotives and rolling stock have been recovered from the countries to which they were exported when new, and there is still much work to be undertaken in restoring items that have been rescued but not yet put into operational order. Like the standard gauge preserved lines, the narrow gauge railways have had to set up workshop facilities to enable them to keep their stock in first class condition, and some rebuilds are so thorough that little remains of the original.

Interest in narrow gauge railways and their preservation is growing, encouraged by the supporting societies for individual lines, and by national organisations such as the Narrow Gauge Railway Society and the Industrial Railway Society. These societies conduct research into the history of the narrow gauge, its locomotives and the old companies, even the smallest hand-worked industrial line. They have considerable archives of material, publish regular journals and have members with a wealth of knowledge on the subject. The secretaries of these societies and their addresses are:

Industrial Railway Society. Honorary Secretary: B. Mettam, 27 Glenfield Crescent, Newbold, Chesterfield, Derbyshire S41 8SF. Website: www.ngrs.org

Narrow Gauge Railway Society. Honorary Secretary: L. Little, 15 Highfields Drive, Old Bilsthorpe, Newark, Nottinghamshire NG22 8SN. Website: www.irsociety.co.uk

FURTHER READING

Billington, M.H. *The Cliffe Hill Mineral Railway.* Plateway Press, 1997.
Boyd, J.I.C. *Festiniog Railway (vols. I and II).* Oakwood Press, 1975.
Boyd, J.I.C. *Narrow Gauge Railways in Mid-Wales.* Oakwood Press, 1970; reprinted 1987.
Boyd, J.I.C. *Narrow Gauge Railways in North Caernarvonshire (vols. I, II and III).* Oakwood Press, 1985.
Cox, D. and Krupa, C. *The Kerry Tramway and Other Light Timber Railways.* Plateway Press, 1992.
Davies, W.J.K. *Light Railways of the First World War.* David & Charles, 1967.
Dean, I., Smith, D. and Neale, A., *Industrial Railways of the South-East.* Middleton Press, 1984.
Harris, Michael. *On the British Narrow Gauge.* Ian Allen, 1980.
Hollingsworth, Brian. *Festiniog Adventure.* David & Charles, 1981.
Johnson, Peter. *Heyday of the Welsh Narrow Gauge.* Ian Allen, 1997.
Kidner, R.W. *Narrow Gauge Railways of Wales.* Oakwood Press, 1947.
Leleux, Sydney. *Leighton Buzzard Light Railway and Associated Quarry Lines.* Oakwood Press, 1969.
Lindsay, Jean. *North Wales Slate Industry.* David & Charles, 1974.
Messenger, Michael J. *British Narrow Gauge Steam.* Bradford Barton, 1973.
Milner, W.J. *The Glyn Valley Tramway.* Oxford Publishing Company, 1984.
Neale, A. *Hunslet Narrow Gauge Locomotives.* Plateway Press, 1995.
Nicholson, Peter. *Industrial Narrow Gauge Railways in Britain.* Bradford Barton, 1973.
Peters, Ivo. *The Narrow Gauge Charm of Yesteryear.* Oxford Publishing Company, 1976.
Robertson, L.S. *Narrow Gauge Railways – Two Feet and Under.* First published 1898; new ed. by Plateway Press, 1988.
Rolt, L.T.C. *Railway Adventure.* David & Charles, 1961.
Taylorson, K. *Narrow Gauge at War (vols. I and II).* Plateway Press, 1996.
Townsend, J.L. *Townsend Hood and the Railways of the Dorking Greystone Lime Co Ltd.* Brockham Museum, 1980.
Turner, Susan. *Padarn and Penrhyn Railway.* David & Charles, 1975.
Webb, Brian. *The British Inernal-Combustion Locomotive 1894–1940.* David & Charles, 1973.

Plateway Press specialises in publications on narrow-gauge and lesser railways and may be contacted at Taverner House, Harling Road, East Harling, Norwich NR16 2QR (www.plateway.co.uk)

PLACES TO VISIT

Intending visitors are advised to find out opening times and check that relevant services are available before travelling.

MUSEUMS AND STEAM CENTRES

Abbey Pumping Station, Corporation Road, Leicester LE4 5PX.
  Telephone: 0116 299 5111. Website: www.leicestermuseums.ac.uk
Almond Valley Heritage Centre, Millfield, Livingstone Village, West Lothian EH54 7AR.
  Telephone: 01506 414957. Website: www.almondvalley.co.uk
Amberley Working Museum, Houghton Bridge, Amberley, Arundel, West Sussex BN18 9LT.
  Telephone: 01798 831370. Website: www.amberleymuseum.co.uk
Biggar Gasworks Museum, Gaswork Road, Biggar, Lanarkshire. Telephone: 01899 221050.
Bressingham Steam Museum, Low Road, Bressingham, Diss, Norfolk IP22 2AA.
  Telephone: 01379 686900. Website: www.bressingham.co.uk
Burlesden Brickworks Museum, Coal Park Lane, Swanwick, Southampton, Hampshire SO31 7GW.
  Telephone: 01489 576248. Website: www.burlesdenbrickworks.org.uk
Corris Railway Museum, Station Yard, Corris Machynlleth, Powys SY20 9SH.
  Telephone: 01654 761303. Website: www.corris.co.uk
Leeds Industrial Museum, Armley Mill, Canal Road, Armley, Leeds LS12 2QF.
  Telephone: 0113 263 7861. Website: www.leeds.gov.uk/armleymills
Llechwedd Slate Caverns, Blaenau Ffestiniog, Gwynedd LL41 3NB.
  Telephone: 01766 830306. Website: www.llechwedd-slate-caverns.co.uk
Llywernog Silver-lead Mine Museum, Ponterwyd, Aberystwyth, Ceredigion SY23 3AB.
  Telephone: 01970 890620. Website: www.silverminetours.co.uk
Morwellham Quay Open Air Museum, Morwellham, Tavistock, Devon PL19 8JL.
  Telephone: 01822 832766. Website: www.morwellham-quay.co.uk

Museum of Lincolnshire Life, The Old Barracks. Burton Road, Lincoln LN1 3LY.
Telephone: 01522 528448. Website: www.lincolnshire.gov.uk
Narrow Gauge Railway Museum, Talyllyn Railway Company, Wharf Station, Tywyn, Gwynedd LL36
9EY. Telephone: 01654 710472. Website: www.ngrm.org.uk
National Slate Museum (National Museum Wales), Padarn Country Park, Llanberis, Gwynedd LL55 4TY.
Telephone: 01286 870 630. Website: www.museumwales.ac.uk
North Ings Farm Museum, Fen Road, Dorrington, Lincolnshire LN4 3QB.
Telephone: 01526 833100. Website: www.northingsfarmmuseum.co.uk
Penrhyn Castle Industrial Railway Museum (National Trust), Bangor, Gwynedd LL57 4HN.
Telephone: 01248 363219. Website: www.nationaltrust.org.uk
Rural Life Centre, Old Kiln Museum, Reeds Road, Tilford, Farnham, Surrey GU10 2DL.
Telephone: 01252 795571. Website: www.rural-life.org.uk

PLEASURE LINES USING FORMER INDUSTRIAL EQUIPMENT
Abbey Light Railway, Bridge Road, Kirkstall, Leeds LS5 3BW (Sundays and Bank Holiday Mondays).
Telephone: 0113 267 5087. Website: www.abbeylightrailway.webs.com
Alford Valley Railway, Alford Station, Alford, Aberdeenshire.
Telephone: 01975 563942. Website: www.alfordvalleyrailway.org.uk
Bala Lake Railway, Llanuwchllyn Station, Bala, Gwynedd LL23 7DD.
Telephone: 01678 540666. Website: www.bala-lake-railway.co.uk
Brecon Mountain Railway, Pant Station, Merthyr Tydfil CF48 2UP.
Telephone: 01685 722988. Website: www.breconmountainrailway.co.uk
East Anglia Transport Museum, Chapel Road, Carlton Colville, Lowestoft, Suffolk NR33 8BL.
Telephone: 01502 518459. Website: www.eatm.org.uk
Ffestiniog Railway, Harbour Station, Porthmadog, Gwynedd LL49 9NF.
Telephone: 01766 516024. Website: www.festrail.co.uk
Great Whipsnade Railway, Whipsnade Wild Animal Park, Dunstable, Bedfordshire LU6 2LF.
Telephone: 01582 872171. Website: www.gwsr.com
Hollycombe Steam Collection, Iron Hill, Liphook, Hampshire GU30 7LP.
Telephone: 01428 724900. Website: www.hollycombe.co.uk
Launceston Steam Railway, St Thomas Road, Launceston, Cornwall PL15 8DA.
Telephone: 01566 775665. Website: www.launcestonsr.co.uk
Leighton Buzzard Railway, Pages Park Station, Billington Road, Leighton Buzzard, Bedfordshire LU7
4TN. Telephone: 01525 373888. Website: www.buzzrail.co.uk
Llanberis Lake Railway, Gilfach Ddu, Llanberis, Gwynedd LL55 4TY.
Telephone: 01286 870549. Website: www.lake-railway.co.uk
Sittingbourne & Kemsley Light Railway, Milton Road, Sittingbourne, Kent ME10 2DZ.
Telephone: 0871 222 1568. Website: www.sklr.net
South Tynedale Railway, The Railway Station, Alston, Cumbria CA9 3JB.
Telephone: 01434 381696. Website: www.strps.org.uk
Talyllyn Railway, Wharf Station, Tywyn, Gwynedd LL36 9EY.
Telephone: 01654 710472. Website: www.talyllyn.co.uk
Teifi Valley Railway, Station Yard, Henllan, near Newcastle Emlyn, Carmarthenshire SA44 5TD.
Telephone: 01559 371077. Website: www.teifivalleyrailway.com
Toddington Narrow Gauge Railway, Toddington Station, Toddington, Cheltenham, Gloucestershire GL54
5DT. Telephone: 01242 621405. Website: www.toddington-narrow-gauge.co.uk
Welsh Highland Heritage Railway, Tremadog Road, Porthmadog, Gwynedd LL49 9DY.
Telephone: 01766 513402. Website: www.whr.co.uk
Welshpool & Llanfair Light Railway, The Station, Llanfair Caereinion, Powys SY21 0SF.
Telephone: 01938 810441. Website: www.wllr.org.uk
West Lancashire Light Railway, Station Road, Hesketh Bank, near Preston, Lancashire PR4 6SS.
Telephone: 01772 815881. Website: www.wllr.net